HORSE IN THE DARK

HORSE IN THE DARK

Poems

VIEVEE FRANCIS

NORTHWESTERN UNIVERSITY PRESS

EVANSTON, ILLINOIS

Northwestern University Press
www.nupress.northwestern.edu

Printed in the United States of America

10 9 8 7 6 5 4 3

Library of Congress Cataloging-in-Publication Data
Francis, Vievee.
    Horse in the dark : poems / Vievee Francis.
      p. cm.
    ISBN 978-0-8101-2840-8 (pbk. : alk. paper)
    1. Texas—Poetry. I. Title.
PS3606.R3653H67 2012
811.6—dc23

                                                          2012000547

The paper used in this publication meets the minimum requirements of the American
National Standard for Information Sciences—Permanence of Paper for Printed Library
Materials, ANSI Z39.48-1992.

For my mother, Elaine Francis

Wir sollen nicht wissen, warum
dieses und jenes uns meistert . . .

We are not to know why,
who, or what masters us . . .

     —Rainer Maria Rilke,
      translation by Kurt Olzmann

Contents

II

III

IV

HORSE IN THE DARK

A hieroglyphics of blister and scuff.
How can *you* know me? Tin and trail,
bray and crocker sack. My gandy-
song—this blue buzz of flies. Sugar
from your palm? No. Give me your fingers.
Under this hair shirt steams the vocabulary
of flesh, crosshatched into meaning.

TRANSFIGURATION

An eight-limbed girl. Hidden under a coat—
a vestigial tail. A grandmother's extra nipples—
a burden, a pleasure. Hair that would be feathers.
Children born in down.

It is not Zeus alone, but the swan who aspires
to shift its shape, pushing forth its chest into a limblike neck,
as the cleft of its feathered end meets a smoother bifurcation,
rounding back its split bill into blue-tinged lips.

The centaur, satyrs, men holy-halved.
Medusa and her head of hair that would sing.

God, beast, or fowl; webbed or hoofed,
what foot moves our own shoe?

Amarillo

Texas Panhandle, 1971

Inland where no seagulls circled,
        no sea, but storms of dust and dust,
heartland: mouthless heart of thistles,
        and waves of sun, of salt, and fish
shimmering in their cans of oil,
        as every surface boiled to rust.

Dusk brought howls of the trickster gods,
        whom cowboys shot and then impaled.
Scruffs of scarecrows lined the fence posts,
        coyotes with their lolling miens,
their smiles now fixed as any man's.

Sons, so like their fathers, strung smaller
        finds: prairie dogs, a Golgotha
of frogs. From that hot panhandle
        the years rose like gulls. O water-
eyed calf lowing from the broom maize—

how singed the yellow world?
How the bluebonnets mock the sea.

STILL LIFE IN YELLOW WITH BROWNS AND BLACKS

Texas Panhandle, 1971

i

The mess of it: sticky-pot black iron always hot a rage of potatoes the burning peppers beans coyote carcasses (necks on a post) mile upon mile pig's feet souring in jars and the dust everything going in crocked together: prairie dog rattler school bus bluets mestizos the son of a cowboy across the street me

and the sun that heats it all to boiling

ii

Early that spring I tongued stamens of honeysuckle and the monarchs thronged the crab-apple tree I watched the pickle making It rained cool as a skull in the earth

Puddle cheekbone kick ball bloodstreak backside windshield windows paddle . . . memory a whirlwind kicking up shells gravel . . .

iii

I imagined my teacher melting I would step lithe as a gingham-skirted Dorothy into the puddle of her skirts her pointer her sneer—

iv

Dunce—the cows eyed me after school I stared back dared them to break the fence Run

Nigra—a crow attacked me one afternoon Escaped from its cage Black bird against a yellow sky

v

Mamma made me sit in it Said, *Sun'll help* Said it would cure my hives my bad nerves I watched the jackrabbits from the porch It was an infestation Town said, *There's as many of them as Mexicans and God help us if the blacks* . . . I wondered what the cowboy's son heard at his dinner table

vi

One with the sun nobody looked directly at me See?

The Plain of Sudden Circumstance

West Texas, 1959

i
Moving west my father
watches the evergreens grow
shorter   until they are
tumbleweeds that surround
a pink house peeling
just one storm after painting,
reminiscent of a torn dress.
It seems to be crying

from a distance. Six miles before
the basket he can see laundry
hanging in the heat
that smells
of biscuits and pork.
The nearest neighbor
is twenty minutes by truck
over the flats and gulfs

of trickster territories
that lead the eye to believe
canyons are mere hoof marks or
snake   holes,
like the one that took
that nosy girl's arm
a season before. Searching
for trouble with a long stick

and burlap,
things will come up on you
quick-like. An Armageddon
of lightning over dog towns.
Next morning
you find their small skeletons
bleached white
as heifer skulls in summer.

ii
Nothing is got easy.
She builds a well in the flour
and cornmeal, then pounds
out the bread.

He watches his mother and learns
to hate her hands, but eats from them
anyway. He tolerates her
along with countless suppers

of cornbread and beans, and beans—
one morning he will decide,
I'm gonna marry
                    a flat woman

—*flat as the Llano.*
His wife will be consoling
in the way nothing will be
hidden. Her certain lack

of mystery.
Comforting as rain
that soothes the droughted
ground.

iii

He saw snow three times one winter,
and it lasted only three weeks,
but froze half a herd of cattle

and the fingers of his mother's
right hand. Some would say
there's significance in that

odd number, those same
would comment on the creek's
swell, and the increase of frogs.

iv

Spiders bind the cactus
and its tinder, so only ferns
sit on his windowsill.

The cemetery and the gardens
are kept by fire ants.
They crawl up a leg as one prays

for a different life, or
a heaven like home,
only free of the rod.

DEVOTION LIKE THIS

The horse winds up, readies itself for the race
it will lose, throat thrust up, air whipped mane
and tongue tight behind its teeth for the rider

it will fail. The horse, as much a hare will run
the course. Jackrabbit quick, mindless love.
Such is the carrot,

novelty in its cheap disguise, trophy, wreath,
the palm that holds the sugar cube. No,
a horse will not give up until an ankle turns,
until a heart bursts from a thistle-filled mouth.
Damn the flag, damn the opening gate,
the bastard and his crop.

How Easily Memory Is Colored

i

Hers is a crayon house with slanted roof, oversized shingles, yellow-brick chimney, wide-eyed windows, shut front door. She draws what she recalls, waxes in the details, colors in the lines. Ask her what happened—she will draw this house.

ii

She slices the world into slats: beige blinds, pink siding. See how simple—

a second sheet will evoke another: a bedroom, eight dolls (and all have their golden heads).

iii

She is ten years old, listening for footsteps, deciphering shadows, checking and checking and checking under the bed. This night will cling, assert itself with the resonance of dull scissors.

iv

She marks her borders with Lincoln Logs. Draws upon a time when small houses loomed large. When all ranches were ranches with plastic horses lined up on the living room floor. When all men were cowboys.

See the rock garden behind the house—

and a crow descends toward a tree. And one white cloud as large as the sun—side by side above the house. Ask her what this means. She will take up a color. She will tell you nothing.

FIELD OF LETTUCE

So much of the row today is given to the ubiquitous
green of iceberg, whose empty head so easily rolls
from bed to simple wrapping,

or the coarser leaves with a history of romaine
in their spines, a bitter output even hares may reject.

So much is tasteless, cold, even Boston, set apart,

overproduced, a species unto itself, so pure (blandly
incestuous) a leaf only the gourmand can taste it.

But *Min* demanded *Lactuca sativa*, a labial vessel —
Min, holding his cock and flail, in right hand and left,
Min, who drank the milk of the lettuce so he could
in turn provide the milk of the Nile, ached for the prickly

variant, the untamed leaf seeding wild among the tamed. O Black
God of Desire, demand again your portion, open this field,
make it give to you what was always yours to have.

THE HEART WILL SCALE THE DEW

Jay Wright

To wake with longing and walk

shoeless through the grass, before the sun

whips its horses through the blades

To grip the bent grass and lap the drops

from the sheath as a horsefly might

flicking its quick-slender tongue

To find you at the threshold

before every bloom withers in the drought

of days without wisteria, without

the dumbstruck, thirsty doves

To embrace

the dun cool of the morning and

its attendant dew as if it were enough

to quench

this wringing out.

GUN OF WISHES

of dreams, gun that opens the mind, gun
of rewards held to the temple, gun
of desire, magic gun,
bloodless and free of catastrophe,
no blood exploding from a whorl
of hair and tissue and skull, gun
that cures, gun of innocence—that's the gun
for me—one that takes out the enemy
with bullets of care, yes, a cautious gun, gun
of considerations, gun you can carry anywhere
and no one minds your gun of good intentions.
Conscious gun, gun of a gun, gun *for you*, gun
for me, trigger-happy nation
of guns,
merry guns, guns a-go-go, guns gone
wild, dancing guns like banjos plucked
hysterical. It's a scream these guns
we believe in. Savior guns, that will set us right,
godly guns, guns at the fount, clean as a whistle,
hot as chickens in a pot, gun for gun's sake, guns
as promised for our own protection, hunting guns,
dove-hunting guns, sweet coo of guns, guns
that will fire to war no more, yes, guns for peace,
kumbaya guns, singing guns—like shooting stars—
a lullaby riddling the night.

BULL SNAKE

I saw the snake before I reached the house—
   There's a town just south that celebrates the snake,
its length of body hanging from my father's fist,
   rounded up, noosed by the head, rattlers and others.
"Bull snake honey."
   Even children peek under rocks and boulders for coils.
"A big one." His rifle leaned against the porch.
   The snakes are used—
But I cannot abide them, poisonous or not—
   for venom, boots, handbags, a seasonal fried supper, belts. . .
It's their undulance—I should have been thrilled to see one dead—
   in some temples a worshipped snake may sate its hunger—
but I screamed and screamed, as if that serpent still held the power
   draped over a fist of figs—
to lift its hissing head, to give me its perilous knowledge.

LOBLOLLY PINE IN A FIELD OF HOLLYHOCKS

There is sweetness, oh yes, there is, like a thin pistil of honeysuckle
gone almost as soon as it's sucked, like lips pursed just so, like a needled pine
with blossoms at its feet and far afield, and the slobbering bees bobbing punch-drunk.
So sweet, to inhale the late afternoon and the slight damp, hint of dew, or the rain
to come, like the rough lick of animals, a whistle, a rude joke in the ear,
trill of dying cicadas, a mouth of sour mead in the quickening day. Dear,
but not innocent, not the purity of some child, no virgin's fount—no,
sweetness like joy must emerge from soil, from the torn fruit grown ripe
to bitter, not the penitent's vision, nor the onanistic ecstasy of a lonely saint,
but the sweetness found in a stain of wine, or the cloy of blood soup, thickening as it cools.

THE COWBOY'S SON

My first love wore chaps
(like his father) roped calves.
Straight backed, bowlegged,
he lived across the street.

Cheeks red as crab apples,
he had a horse and two brothers.
I had a brown mare named Trixie.
She lived on my grandmother's

land a few hundred miles east,
far from tumbleweeds, dog towns,
the sun like the round hole
of a lariat over a cow's neck.

She lived where there were more
trees, more shade, but just
as many men with rifles.
Rifles killed a mad crow that year—

loosed from a bird's cage
at the Conoco—see I remember.
I was eight when it landed.
The cowboy's son was ten or eleven.

Black feathers rained as it rose
from my nape, the crab-apple tree
dropped its fruit. The crow
soon fell dead on the sidewalk.

Paper said, *Year of the Jackrabbit.*
Paper said, *In-fes-ta-tion.*
Teachers said, Parents said,
one then two, then the whole damned

town — My daddy talked — *grown folk's*
business, but I understood. After
Judy Lynn signed my record album
at the rodeo (her lips — angel pink).

I waited by the gates.
He never spoke.

A leap—

               into a hush of bluebonnets.

Alone, I divide,

        split in two. Hare's math, child's magic.

My halves become whole then split again.

Noses wet, timorous, haunch to haunch,
we nuzzle, we

             gambol over

                  the dandelions,

wind through thistle, thistle soft as lettuce heads,
we bound through sudden green, boundless earth.

THE CONJUNCTIONS

Texas Panhandle, 197_

i
How easily memory is colored
Brown cheekbones

Red kick ball
Bloodstreak

Window
Sunray

Wheel
Aisle

Bus
See

Car
Car

Glare
March

Monarchs
Traintracks

Spring of glass
Spring of feathers

Blackbirds falling red
Broken blue eyed flowers

They walked us outside during gym past the wreck.   The sun was shining then.
The sun was shining then. They walked the entire third grade class past the wreck. I
stood in the middle of the line. I stood out. Clear as the sun.   Omnipresent. Small
dark me. Like a kick ball. We played during gym. Ball in orbit. Kick her. She's it.
        Teacher played. The bus stood tilted. Teacher omnipresent as the sun.
But I got all the attention. Split back to middle. Not praise. But attention   is almost
the same. It puts you in the center. A sun of my own. Dark center of a bright universe.
Inverse. I stood outside watching. Lopsided   front to middle. They marched us
by the wreck before snack. Before we had to mount our own buses. Buses that didn't
stand lopsided in a field. Buses that drove straight down straight town roads.   A
kick ball. Red god of the field. The sun   didn't help. It stopped nothing. We could
see the blood on the windows. Fingerprints pressed into glass. They marched us   by
the wreck to honor the fallen.   The sun was shining then. See?   The sun
stopped nothing. It didn't help the driver of the car see   the bumper of the
bus. Tilted to the left. Small, dark   me.   Huge, bloody bus. Teacher played. There
was a principal. He had the teacher   march us by the wreck in rows of two.
Attention is not praise but   almost. So close. It puts you in the center. Like the
bus in the middle of a field, bent as if hit by some huge paddle. Broken   center of a
white universe.   The sun no God to speak of.

HORSE IN THE DARK

for Paula Roper

Brown as a mule, I stomped
through the flocking geese
who thought themselves swans—

but a mule knows its opposite
and so did I. They were no swans.
A horse can be broken by such

beauty. A horse may follow it
down a slope that will slice its hooves.
Beauty, like a restless man in a tall hat,

a wandering boy with teeth
white as if he had never known meat,
or the score of water over stones.

I leapt up for the rain cloud
shaped like a darker horse,
failed a too-tall fence believing

a horse could be loved more
and ridden less, until we fell apart,
the horse I was and I.

We who had prayed for a heaven
of toothless grass and barley, how
did we untwine? When

did my long face pull itself back
into this form? How
did words replace neigh?

Two legs took my four.
And I, freed of my horse-self
who lay dead to the world,

ran through the clover. On two legs

                                        ran and ran . . .

I WILL BE THERE FOREVER AND WAS NEVER THERE AT ALL

Deep East Texas, 1967

A wheel rolls muddy through the field.
A tick is sucked from the knee.
Men, with their boiled egg skin, say,
"Hot today," swat flies with feed ads.
The bottomland has its snakes, and children.
A man with swollen knuckles sells ribbon cane,
offers a finger-suck sweet and dusty as a teat.
Overalls dangle from a line, strung on rotted frames.

Here: the earth suddenly rich where history molders
under the mounds, brass, peashot, skull,
while above the blue-eyed grass seeds wild.
This field has reclaimed itself, tracks reduced to *this*

thin trace, the way that coon slipped from her limb
—years ago—into the hound's mouth. Who would believe it?

IN PRAISE OF SOLOMON, WHO PREFERRED THE NIGHT

for Matthew

and its creatures that rose from the sand to speak,
who brought before him their cases, scorpion and snake,

trusting his discretion, and knowledge of the law.
And the stars in their illimitable number where all things

possible are justly made so. And knowing this: Solomon
lived without fear and took to his side Sheba, who spoke

in tongues to her camels burdened with myrrh, and the lambs
whose wool was plucked to make Solomon a cloak

for the cool of the evenings, and a counterpane
for their bed. With Sheba alone

he walked through the garden, which was not Eden—
but neither was ashamed in their skins.

He and a woman whose knowledge of beasts
was as boundless as his understanding of man,

and each preferring the equanimity of night
whose darkness encompasses all.

DE RERUM NATURA

> How beautiful the Centaurides are, even where they
> are horses; for some grow out of white mares . . .
>
> —Philostratus the Elder

i

I named my horse Trixie
and was half-afraid to ride her,
brown as me and equally skittish,
but once upon her, we were joined
at the withers. I was no less
than Hylonome.

ii

According to Lucretius, *Each man struggles to escape himself*

though a horse is discussed in better terms
than a mule. From what does the mule run?
the ass of her mother? the stomping rage
of her father?

iii

Lamentation: Trixie died,
I don't remember how. I remember
her girth, the comfort of knowing
all that she was was mine.

iv

Zora's claim: *De nigger woman is de mule* . . .
capable of speech,
meaning: a beast no more or less

v

Like any child, of course, I loved horses
more than myself, and believed Trixie
spoke to me in a language all our own.

vi

I saw *Francis* on television, I said, *Ma*,
I'm a mule, we're mules, quick, come see.

vii

Impossibility:
the verdict of Lucretius,
who could not have imagined me.

MARRED

In our darkness angels come to us

marred as plowmen, bowed as the earth,

    arms and backs a-run with keloids like creeks,

        and hillocks—the topography of accidents—

          toes lopped, half a hand, stammer of a ten-toothed mouth,

      noses flattened as if hit by the flat of a spade, as we

  blindly weep, ignorant of the evidence of their trials:

    lesions, boils, a tumor pressing bulbous from the shoulder,

                  burns whipped through skin like comets through
a night sky.

PEACHES

What do they call me?

— Nina Simone

Biscoe   grew in my grandmother's backyard. Pink blooms littered the stoop.

O'Henry   blushing, hairless. So many suitors. Who doesn't love *peaches*?

Summer Pearl   white-fleshed. At birth my grandmother could have passed, was passed off by her father to a husband twenty years older.

Indian Blood   her husband's claim. Oklahoma strike through the skin. No documents to verify, muscat riddling the tongue.

White Lady   in a crimson coat. That winter, I said, to the woman she had picked cotton for, "My grandmamma's name isn't 'gal,' it's Ma'am, Ma'am."

Early Freedom   plucked from the low-lying limb. A story told at last. Red lipped from the rendering. Her own grandmother, freed two and a half years too late.

Garnett Beauties and Red-Cheeked Belles   picnic in the Texas heat. Juneteenth fare: a white-feathered chicken fried into celebration.

FISHING HOLE

East Texas, 1974

The blade went straight through the turtle's belly.
My first catch of the day.
Standing under a tree with my pole
I called out to my grandmother.
She said, *Good girl, now wait just a minute.*
Came back with a stripe-handled butcher's knife,
said, *Here girl, kill it quick.*   No.
Go on. It'll make a good supper. No.
The blade pierced the soft underside, so quick—

        there was its hilt and wet inches
of blade sticking out. *Pull the knife out, stop acting up.*
She stood above me. I pulled at the knife.
The turtle's legs wiggled. *Pull.* Another wiggle.
She finally bent and freed the knife herself.
It made a sucking sound. She sucked her teeth,
said, *Git!* I got in the truck bed, laid on my back.

Granny Peaches snapped the chicken's neck, just like that.
Don't remember the bird's name. I coveted the white meat.
Do remember the taste—if not the feet, or beak
that must have been cleaved, or the grayish bones I'm sure I sucked.
It fought. The white feathers fell slowly as the black.
Now, I keep her recipe. She fried it in flour and blood.

What are we to the trees
whose roots embrace us?

THE RULE OF THE FOREST

is to take the body in,
to wrap tendrils 'round
and let the leaves fall wet
to the ground above
like a mother's worried palm
to the forehead. The branches
shiver, *tsk, tsk,* and the wind
seems to push through to stroke
the naked arms, as if to say,
There, there my dear, it's over.
And it is. The earth below
the body yields to its weight,
and the closed eyes feel the press
of a sky of moss.
The ants march over, under,
through and around,
their mandibles never still.
So the body gives way, to mulch
after madness, after the mean
force no longer propels
it forward, but down and down.

STILL LIFE WITH ANOTHER GRANDFATHER, MASONS, AND A PIE TIN UNDER THE BED

East Texas, 1997

Peaches buried him by the railroad tracks
on the same side where they had lived.
A gathering of hob-toed wives and grave men
leaned in just enough to hear the preacher.
A girl with her thumb stuck in a puckered mouth.
Gregarious boys whose curious indifference led them
to chase hounds.

        We waited in the clearing.
Wooden shacks poked through the tall pines.
I bounced from the ball of one patent-leathered foot
to the other, shaking off red ants and clay.

The pallbearers wore white aprons and carried staffs
taller than themselves. Their voices rose
in mummer's rounds above the casket.

My grandmother had outlived two men,
one two decades her senior. She had kept a pie tin
filled with ammonia under the bed for their good luck.
He left everything to his children.
He left her nothing but alone.

EULOGY WITH FEAST AND A TALL BLACK MAN ON BASS

East Texas, 2005

Pepper sauce on field peas.
He was dark as a purple hull.

Pears gone to sweet vinegar.
What she would have desired.

Raisin pie and collards.
He stood narrow and slick-haired.

Everything you grew and then some.
Tall, wind-bent.

O Woman for whom there was no rest but this.

Fryers and neck bones.
He had that kind of attitude.

The Bowie sisters had wide laps.
Song of pine.

O Woman for whom this is all.

Such good women bury their husbands in winter.
Song of needles.

They spread the feast, pickled cornucopia
He opened his mouth,

held me like a child,
and wailed.

the bus crashed, no—a car crashed
into the bus—I felt my teeth on a window
—that was not my mouth—
my mouth was in my head in a field
of thistle and bonnets—I saw the blood-
stained metal rods separating
tops of windows from bottoms
—that is the window I remember—
they walked us by the wreck—
the entire third grade—did I tell you?
—what you can't forget you tell—
or die in it—now—I have told you—
I saw the windows were eyes looking —
the yellow bus stood in a field—
quiet—as if—nothing had hap—

the eyes were upon me—
all the red-rimmed eyes—
I stood in the field—
in the car my mother waiting—
blew the horn—blew the horn—

PIG HEAD IN A PLASTIC SACK

with eyes plucked from sockets,
like pecans sewn into a flour bag,
ribbon cane syrup in a lid-stuck tin,
calf legs half sealed in a womb swollen shut.
Pray me out. Pray me out.
Is it bright? Can you hear me?

III

Before Crushing the Heads of Her Sleeping Boys She Heard the Breeze A-Whispering

East Texas, 2005

God is in the pine
the close woods dark   *hush*
as the hills at night   *hush*
a rolling line of treetops
purpling the dusk
I burn the trash in the side yard
then scrub the bathroom tiles
on my knees   *somebody's callin'*
with rags cut from towels
as I was taught   *my name*
not missing any corners
not a hair from the dog
or the scuff of a little shoe
A bucket of boiling water
and pine oil kills
the odors of the day
even the toilet brush won't
escape—I dip it in the pail water
and take it 'round three times
before putting it back
on its plastic post
I clean in the evening   *hush*
after the boys are in bed   *hush*
and their clatter quiets
to snores I don't hear
once the doors are closed
I open the windows then
to dry the floor
and a breeze pushes through

pines into the house   *somebody's callin'*
and I know yes I know   *my name*
He's talking to me   *hush*
I'm back on my knees   *hush*
in the kitchen now   *somebody's callin'*
I swab the linoleum with my hair
to let Him know I'm not too proud
There's no one coming home tonight
I recite the Psalms as I wring my braids
then start the dusting
The breeze picks up   *my name*
I go out to sweep
gravel from the porch and—
see the rocks? I know   *O my Lord*
it's time to climb the tree-line   *O my Lord*
just like Moses   *What shall I do?*

KILLING JIM MITCHELL

Texas, 1910

Like a mouse jarred by a screaming girl,
he stood openmouthed in my stare,
as if the heat from my body just in from the field
had melded his feet to the ground. I wanted to explain,
to justify the low stand, *the cane was wet, too wet to grow,*
it sunk, bowed its head in defeat.
I couldn't make my share. Could the rain be held
against me? He took my exasperation for rage.
I took his fear as insult, and wanted to break
his hold over me, only his hold—

He hit her in the back of the head   Truth—finds its own coarse measure
Not long out of diapers I wore purple hot pants   danced a funky chicken
There was the boogaloo and my aunt's wig that went over her hair
I knew men even then   I had uncles   And a father

We jumped high in the living room   our lives a quickstep
When I held her in my arms did I do any good?
She was hip   too cool   a Saturday night cigarette
a bone-handled pistol in the panty drawer   Say it louder—

I was proud   I held my head high with my Sally-legged aunt
I kicked my heels and my uncle laughed
He had a western name
This was Texas   a man's world   but women raised these men out of cotton

out of dust   Bred longhorns and bullshit   She could shoot   but she didn't
She said   Sing it baby   *Please, plea*— I got down on my knees
and cradled her son's head in my small arms   Out of memory
the thread of truth   a red daisy chain   blood running down a back

He hit her again
I was wearing my purple hot pants   ones that matched hers   or
I was in my pajamas holding my cousin's head in my arms
covering his eyes his mouth with my flat chest   my fingers in his hair

hair red as his mother's   Coarse   As in unrefined   She wore a wig
that fell off her head
He screamed "Fat bitch"   She cried "Don't go"   and let her pony-legs go
to sticks thin as a bluebonnet stem   Texas flower   weed

When I held her in my arms it did no good   When my mother held her
        in her arms she did not come back
I said "Don't go"   She said *I'm black*—I sang *Say it loud*
He said "Black bitch" It was a boogaloo   it had been danced before

My uncle laughed his laugh   It fell like a wig to the floor
        He threw back his head
        conked   slick as a razor blade
I'm saying it

the way truth comes out when it's been held too long
to your chest in a boy's cries   a boy who will grow
into his father's shoes   Dance of generations
Cotton-eyed marshals   Green-eyed brown men

She said "You can't trust men like that"   Turned me around
said "Do your dance girl   sing that song"
                        She could shoot   but didn't
Someone else did   I'm saying

in a bar years and miles up the road he fell
like a wig hitting the floor   Juke joint   Gin-stomp
James Brown always spinning He was big stuff
in a slim suit   Cool as Saturday night he fell
                                hair flawlessly coiled.

The sound   of blue
appears   disheveled
from a distance mud-ridden
a sweating tramp   damp
as cotton in dew
a tear in the fabric
closer
like the quilt of an overcast sky
blown down   The sound presses
into the wide flare of an old man's nostrils
closer
it smells like peaches and piss
knuckles in an egg jar   knuckles
rounding a mouth harp
blowing   the sound wide as a holler   a hoop

a skirt flung up and   over the head

love loosed from the brine   smells

the way blood set to heat makes you hungry

Open your mouth   let the salt in   the moan out

O   can you feel it honey?   the linoleum hitting your knees

the sound of a bone snapping   a bone broken

and set with plywood   You'll walk with a cry

a cry like rain on tin   just overhead now   the music

in this white-framed house

with its rust roof and chicken-scatter and the sound

O the sound   It's holding you tight

means to stay.

Anti-Pastoral

i

How often have I spoken of the thistle,
the honeysuckle, the blistering bees?
How often have I asked *how*? I've grown tired
of my questions. And you've grown tired
of the limits of my language. I hate this measure
of memory, the constant return to the creek, the field,
the sundering South. I want release from the pasture
of my youth, from its cows and cobs in the mouth.
Forgive my tiresome nostalgia. Forget it.
Let me forge a fissure between what was and is.
I have no accent. You would not know where I was from
if I didn't keep reminding you. Look at my city
shoes crunching through the new snow
on the sidewalk. Not a blade of grass anywhere.

ii

Which is not to say, Praise the urban, privilege the shadow
of the alley over the shade beneath a tree, or the average sky-
scraper over the clearing.

iii

Not in a surfeit of emotion, but in its thoughtful
consideration, later, when natural rage, through meditation,
may be pulled as milk through an udder, into a purer stream
—this is how Wordsworth would have it,
not red-eyed and trembling, but clearheaded,
the tempest assuaged. Can you believe that?
Easy to say from some green-lined walking trail,
but this is a city, and here is an old woman

on the curb, broken easily as a wafer she might have
had with her iced tea later this evening. Here is a reason
to prefer whiskey over a cow's poor offering. Whiskey,
essential as water, worthy of pain and erasure.
And she is one of many, so I drink to her and her and her—

there was darkness there—and light too—
but mostly the dark moving pine to pine
beneath the porches in the never opened
back closets the stuck drawers behind
the stove settled into its grease.

Lift the jars lining the pantry shelves and
there the dark will be in the fermented pears
in the bluet honey enough darkness to string
a bee box to draw the hounds "just so" dark
"listenhere" dark "watchyourself" dark
"I'll be damned" "come and get it"
"besttoleaveitalone" "hitch your skirt up"
belly lift and knees down darkness under
the skin where a tick burrows either way
for better or worse so it goes here it comes
no way around the darkness dark inherent
forever and amen ever.

TUG

I hate her hands, the nails curved
overgrowth hard as a coon's claw.
She grabs my wrists, shouts, *Don't go,*
digs in at the vein. I feels the coarse grip
of the cotton picker, pecan plucker,
the knobbed knuckles so damaged
they bloom, making her fingers
immovable as the fingers
of the newly laid dead.

I pry loose her suddenly animate hand.
What desperate surge makes her close
the ruined appendage around my own?
Next week I'll come back, kiss her forehead
and tell her I stayed all night. Like I used to
decades ago during summer visits, curled up
like a roly-poly against her small belly
in the big bed, letting her fingers plait my hair,
her wrist, the occasional visitor
stroking my cheek.

ANTEATER AT THE DALLAS ZOO

The ants work together toward their end,
toward continuance, never see Death's approach,
believe the shadow of its body to be an overcast sky,
and its legs, gnarled as bark—merely tree trunks.
The extension of its nose—only a falling vine,
until a sticky frond takes them up, one
by one, into a heaven of the interior,
which is to say, of course, a hell.

Daddy slaughtered the hog right there in the side yard,
and it hurt to see it, but that won't stop me from eating.
Come Thanksgiving, I'll dip a bit of ham in Jackson's
Ribbon Cane Syrup, and pop it inside a biscuit.
When it's time to celebrate, something dies.
When something dies, we take it with the sweet.

Take my cousin Gerald—he left us last summer,
a tractor accident. We were cousins by marriage, but
friends by choice, so I cried more than when I broke my leg
jumping off the front porch—bone snapped clean through.
After the funeral, as the Lord is my witness,
those were the best potato pies I ever had.

Yesterday, where the yellow pines meet the creek,
that boy on the other side of the property line
helped bring his daddy's cattle in. I watched him watch
me standing in a field littered with cow's corn,
my head tilted just enough to let him know I was
curious. He left a scarlet ribbon tied to the barbed wire.
My heart skipped quicker than a swallow's when I found it.
Now I'm wondering what throat's going to open?
I need to warn him—the wheel never rusts, never stops.

O, I loved the cane.
I'd take a piece, cut
with a pocket knife
from the stalk so like
bamboo, and bite
hard into the sweet matter.
Let it fill my mouth
with the life I had:
enough dust to choke on,
and the milk shot warm
and bloodstained
into the pail.

OF CENTAUROMACHY

Every man his own horse

Ridiculous cloy—lavender
on the precipice, the eucalyptus scent
of the loblolly pines rising sharply
from the valley, the mane of a woman
bathed in wine-warm water—
enough sweetness to make a man
swallow his tongue, to make a horse
forget himself.

So, how to halve it, parse haunches
from the equally hirsute flesh that hides
Adam's ribs and a mount's heart? You
—easily desired and desiring, loneliness
being as irresistible as love—want
release from your own Mythology,
from the buck of desire, the orgy of days—

but a finger run over the withers
draws the beast whose tale you'd deny.
Fool for blood and scent, wine and the brink,
spending every arrow in the quiver,
your story is no minor romp

in the high grass, take up the lyre,
then from the jut let your song canter
down like seed into the dale below.
O Chiron, you were meant to sing,
and so lay down your bow.

THE BEACH STILL HAS ITS DANGERS

Galveston, 2008

Robert Hayden's white horses, the ones Jemima saw,
leap right up onto the beach where I stand.

Each has two faces and each face seems
to rise from the foam.

Are you in the cabinet?
they ask in one voice.

Too stunned to answer, I don't.

They stamp their hooves,
make muck of the shoreline.

No, I say, I am not in the Cabinet.
I am no Secretary. No politico,

and isn't that topical?
Topical as Ever. You look like Jemima.

They raise and shake their tower heads.
Starfish, flotsam, and bones fall at my feet.

I feel my time is short.

What did you ask Jemima?
For the recipe, of course . . .

Of course.

WATER, WHILE NOT LOVE, IS SO SIMILAR

It will take you under if it can. The world
is more water than love, and water is
indifferent to our crisis. My dear,

it will not save you, and any comfort
you gain, well, it is your own
imagination pulling the blanket up
over you, warming the milk.

And while the sea may feel all that lives
within it, it is neither angered nor
concerned. We cannot fathom it.

And it, in all its wetness, still
or wild, would fill our mouths,
our noses, our lungs without
considering the consequences,
not once, not ever.

At the Lethe I Met My Mother and She Did Not Know Me

She thought I was a stranger come to attack
her (or my father —
since I wear his face).

A ladle was perched at her lips.
Had she drunk, or was she about to?
I knocked it from her hand. To save her,

I took her in my arms.
She was repulsed, fought me off
(she had always hated to embrace).

She was more terrified than usual.
I said, *Mother, it's me.*
She said, *I know* (but she did not).

She thought I was a bill collector.
She thought she owed everyone.
You owe me, she cried.

She thought I was a census taker
and shut the door. Her eyes fell
like blinds.

I pounded on her chest, begged,
Mother, let me in. She said, *Water*,
but closed her lips.

To save her, I put the ladle to mine.

THE SEA HORSE'S LAMENT

In the mangroves a father gives birth,
as his father did, and his father—
the contraction of thirteen million years,
from the distant hills of Slovenia to this night
in the shoals. A thousand bobbing heads
of fry will be swept into the cold currents.
Some will die in the shiver. Others—
will be eaten by creatures with hardier spines.
O forlorn patria, who remains by a father's side?
How can we go on through the tides to bear more?

On the Way to Round Rock

2003

An ice machine rusts in the middle of a field.
A bull skull. A dog too old, too weary to run.
The boy on the tractor watches butterflies float
toward the half-dead trees along CR 122.
There is a treeless split a half mile up
where buzzards sit on the fence post waiting
for what will wander up to Yegua Creek to die.
The same sun that blistered the shirtless toddlers
last summer, further browns a standing trailer.
A cow chews cud and ignores the tractor
(more rust than tractor) while the boy talks to himself.
Across the way, a girl sings and wipes down pews.
Her song (sweet as funeral cakes) moves
over the molting carpet, then through the open doors.

Morning, the glistening
grass draws me into the day,
as if new meant separate
from the day before—

and I, having that human part
that can be transfixed by bauble or blade,
limp out again, a believer,
into memory's emerald glint.

PITY THE SWINE ITS SUCCULENCE

Pig, pig, repellent chop, rutting hock,
sow of sorrows, hated by half
the known world, cut down in your prime
by the rest. You are despised
whether eaten or not. Filthy, fat,
enticing as the apple in your mouth.

Cows when uneaten are revered.
A clover path lay before them, as they
in dim-eyed indifference munch
their cud. For those who do partake,
bovines are admired for their marbling
fat—

and no one yells DIRTY CHICKEN—
though the chicken
pushes its beak through small clods
of its own shit to find an undigested seed.

So why detest the hog in its pen?

Can we deny the perfume
of its renderings waking us
from a dream of fields.
Or how its ampleness sustains
us in godlike manifestations,
taking on whatever we need it to be;
holiday ham, enemy of nations.

Pity the swine its succulence,
the delectable fat that will not be
denied, tempting us into gluttony,
into shame. The sweet pink flesh
hidden as desire and its object is
so often hidden, just below the bristle.

STILL LIFE WITH SUMMER SAUSAGE, A BLADE, AND NO BLOOD

East Texas, 198_

I remember, we walked (we didn't walk)
from the farmhouse to the store in Palestine
(we drove the truck, got out, went in).
The storefronts hadn't changed since
my father was a child. He grabbed saltines from the bin
(he bought a box) and he bought some sausage.
We walked (yes, then we walked) around town
as we ate (he shared). He gave me some summer
sausage, cut with his pocket knife. I pulled the pieces
from the point of the blade. I knew (knew)
nothing would happen (though he was silent)
to alter this memory. We were together
in Texas and we ate and walked in silence
and it felt like smiling, like skipping, like saying,
"Daddy" and him not minding, not minding at all.

OLD FARMER

Texas Hill Country, 2003

You are in the open room, on the old couch,
and will not or cannot remember me. You smile
and joke with the stranger eating meat at your table.

Strangeness in a woman means she can't be trusted,

so you keep your distance on the other side of the room.
Laughter is, in the end, *Devil's Medicine*, but you can't help it,
you laugh. Because my father is miles away I laugh too.

Once, I thought you and he were the same man.
You beat him into manhood. He beat me into the common
turns: fat aunt, mad martyr. Why make it pretty? I'm not.

I planned this visit to make peace with my place,
with my cotton-picker's knuckles, my teeth
sharp as a coon's up a tree.

Brutal Paw,
I have come to give you what for,
but you have grown short and hunched in my absence.

The plow that furrowed your brow will soon break your plot.
Though you have not forgotten *how fit for sin all women are,*
you grin, and I laugh at this trick of fate.

Grandma says, "He doesn't know you anymore."
And I must remember to tell your son, my father,
that he too may one day forget himself, and be forgiven.

what I
have, for,
I think
you can
eat it,
something
red, but
not blood,
sweeter,
like juice,
sweeter
than duck's
blood, though
that is
sweet, yes,
candy-
like, and
good, but
not red
heated,
no, this
is cool,
and fits
in a palm
held up,
or on
a good
teacher's
desk, there
is a

story
I read,
where A
was for
evil,
for long-
ing and
knowledge,
a less-
on learned
and lost,
A is
for, is
for, I
forget

ARS POETICA

I keep rifles in the front closet.
        Trespassing can be a glance.

A good shot,
        I practice with bottles, bull's eyes.

I cross the line where the fence breaks,
        where the wood falls in unintended directions,

and prepare an offensive
        before any repair.

I know the value of my property.
Ungloved, I place the barbed wire.

STILL LIFE IN WHITE WITH FREE MEN AND DUST

for George Francis Jr., 1922–2009

In the Hill Country, German settled—the farmers
make sausage, cattlemen cut bulls into steers,

men call their hard women "sweet,"
name their ranches after mothers and wives.

It's quiet out there. Quiet in the stone houses.

Walk in for food without boots, or a hat,
people will wonder, may offer to buy you both.

If your father belts you, you won't cry, not a sound.
If a man decides God's not listening, hangs himself,

people will say, *umph*, then sip a lemonade,
bite into a melon. *Yes, indeed.*

Germans taught the runaways and the newly freed
to read. They too had run. Understood in their way.

You might find yourself in a field of some sweet flower
there, where the honey tastes of dust and sorghum.

You might be buried on a hill
in a land where work is everything,

where the red ants will make quick work of you.

DELIVERING THE BEAST

There will be no hand waiting.
No one will expect you. Your movement
will not be a rising action, but
a slide across, which will be no easier
than a climb up the displeased face of a mountain.
You may find your neck in a bone scarf
but believe you are running up a green
embankment. I'm telling you,
there will be no soft gloves.
You will trip over your own feet
in your will to go farther, in your Hölderlin-
like reach. And you will do it alone,
                                        my friend.
Which will make you demented, and unstoppable.

There was a wind—this is always the start, the breath of chaos, the mouth against another's, the overanimate inhabiting what would otherwise remain cool to the touch, unable to rouse itself to action. I said, I might die for lack. I said, I am so contained I am the container. I said, *break me.* There was possibility, which was itself an action. The breeze picked up. I felt the chaff lift from the wheat. The wide expanse of me widening still even as I was shaped. Then the lip of insistence, the air moved through a hollow, over tongue and tooth. And I, now, with a mouth to speak, openly moan as chaos reshapes itself in my own form, feel myself quicken to its will, itself in my hands.

TO BE PEGASUS

А вам, в безвременьи летающим

And you, flying in timelessness

—Osip Mandelstam, "The Sky Is Pregnant with the Future"

Ahead,

the horse is the rider,

the field it runs, the crop.

Such a horse,

runs toward who knows where,

forgets itself,

flies on its legs.

Acknowledgments

I would like to thank the following:

my husband, poet and writer Matthew Scott Olzmann, whose boundless care and companionship gives me the courage to look forward,

the Afrillachians whose acceptance freed me to look back,

and my Texas line, immediate and extended.

For his largesse as friend and poet, Gregory Pardlo, and for their generosity of spirit: Scott Hightower, Janice Harrington, Thylias Moss, and A.Van Jordan,

as well as Andrea Beauchamp, Megan Levad, Irma Watt, Scheherazade Parrish, and the Café 1923 family in Hamtramck.

For their critical assessments and support while writing this book I thank Cyrus Cassells, Michael Collier, Nicholas Delbanco, Lorna Goodison, Laura Kasischke, Ray McDaniel, Eileen Pollack, and Keith Taylor; readers Jamaal May and Tommye Blount; the Rona Jaffe Foundation; the Kresge Arts Foundation; and my 2003 Callaloo cohorts,

as well as the editorial staff at *Callaloo* and Dr. Charles Rowell, whose affirmation and kind counsel were pivotal to the development of this book.

I thank the editors and staff of Northwestern University Press for their patience and guidance; the staff of Cave Canem, Alison Meyers, Cornelius Eady, and Toi Derricotte, whose community inspires me; and finally, Parneshia Jones and Adrian Matejka for believing in my work.

The following poems and short prose pieces appeared first in these publications: "Smoke Under the Bale" in *Best American Poetry 2010*, and with "Amarillo," "Horse in the Dark," and "Still Life with Summer Sausage, a Blade, and No Blood" in *Callaloo*, and in *Angles of Ascent:A Norton Anthology of Contemporary African American Poetry*; "The Plain of Sudden Circumstance" in *The Detroit Metro Times*; "Gun of Wishes" in *Fishhouse* (audio), in *Boxcar Review*, and in *Best of the Web*; "Loblolly Pine in a Field of Hollyhocks" in the *Indiana Review*; "I Will Be There Forever and Was Never There At All" in *Renaissance City*; "Fishing Hole," "The Sea Horse's Lament," "The Beach Still Has Its Dangers," and "On The Way to Round Rock" in *Sou'wester*; "Say It, Say It Any Way You Can" in *Rattle* and *Callaloo*; "Sugar and Brine" in *Concho River Review*.